Border Voices
II

An Anthology
by Major Poets
and
San Diego Students

ISBN 0-9640275-1-8

J.F. Webb
P.O. Box 191
San Diego, CA 92112

Cover Art: Veronica Cunningham
Book Design and Layout: Sandra J. Welch

CALIFORNIA COUNCIL FOR THE HUMANITIES

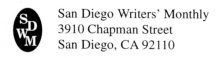

San Diego Writers' Monthly
3910 Chapman Street
San Diego, CA 92110

CONTENTS

The Major Poets

The Student Poems

DEDICATION

"And gladly wolde he lerne, and gladly teche."
— Prologue, *The Canterbury Tales*

This book is dedicated to Dr. Dave Hermanson of the San Diego Unified School District, whose commitment to excellence and to today's youth was instrumental in developing the Border Voices project.

Marina Morrow / Grade 12, Scripps Ranch High

"Jazz" / Ramsey Green / Grade 10, Point Loma High

INTRODUCTION

My heart is like a
jaguar running fast
as it can
in the magic cave
of blue wonder

Melinda Montag
Grade 5, John Adams Elementary

It's been a remarkable year for poetry. In Britain, according to Reuters News Service, doctors have begun prescribing poetry instead of pills to people suffering from anxiety and depression.

"Poetry is infinitely superior to any tablets; just like music, it is therapeutic," said Dr. Alexander Macara, chairman of the British Medical Association. Macara noted a recent study that found a few lines of Wordsworth, Keats or Browning enabled patients to do without pills — a finding that, he acknowledged, "the pharmaceutical industry might not like."

In San Diego, the Border Voices Poetry Project, in cooperation with numerous community organizations and philanthropists, has begun "prescribing" poetry to both children and adults as they face the exciting but sometimes troubling challenges of life in an increasingly diverse society. The results have been astonishing. Not only have our children discovered their own powerful and honest voices — voices which you can "hear" by exploring the pages of this book — but adults too have become intrigued by the possibilities for personal development and self-expression implicit in the art of poetry.

For example, Border Voices — in cooperation with the Metropolitan Transit District and *The San Diego Union-Tribune*, among others — has been putting poems by San Diego students as well as major poets on the city's buses and trolleys. Here is what one patron of the trolley system had to say about that:

> It was just this morning, as I was coming into work on the trolley and I was beginning to get that "glazed" look in my eyes, that I noticed the posters. I had to fight the urge of pointing them out to everyone around me so they could share my excitment. I also had to control myself by not running up and down the car reading all the posters. I'll probably ration myself to one or two a day.

The excitement was also tangible at the Padres home opener last year when Fred Moramarco read a poem about the Padres' stellar outfielder, Tony Gwynn. More than 40,000 people roared with surprised delight as Moramarco's fresh rhythms captured the beauty of baseball and a great player. The same excitement could be found in classrooms throughout the county. One Mexican-American teen, for example, had been thinking of dropping out of school until he won a prize at last year's Border Voices Poetry Fair in Balboa Park. Now he's going on to college.

It is a credit to our community that these results, as well as the dedication of hundreds of supporters, has captured national and even international attention. Articles on Border Voices have appeared in mainstream and literary publications in both the United States and Mexico. L.A.'s Jack Grapes, editor of *ON THE BUS* magazine, summarized one reason for this interest: "You have had enormous success with the Border Voices Poetry Project. There is nothing like it in L.A. or anywhere else that I know of."

Last year's poetry fair drew hundreds of people to Balboa Park to hear nationally recognized poets like Philip Levine, Gary Soto and Marilyn Chin. On March 11-12 of this year, the Pulitzer Prize-winning poet Gary Snyder will be joined by the Native American/African American poet Ai, Fred Moramarco, Juan Felipe Herrera, Sandra Alcosser and others at the Organ Pavilion in the park, where — with a mixture of music and powerful words — they will entertain the crowds. Thanks to Border Voices contributors, there will be no admission charge.

That's the big picture. It's an exciting one, but no more exciting than the poems by major poets and San Diego students who are in this book. Each of the major poets who will be appearing at this year's fair donated a poem for this anthology, and they're as marvelous as you would expect. But the student poems are perhaps even more marvelous, for, as one parent said, "Who would have thought our children had so much in them?"

But they do.

J. F. Webb
Director, Border Voices Poetry Project
Co-director, New Voices in the Humanities
Assistant News Editor,
The San Diego Union-Tribune

ACKNOWLEDGEMENTS

Both this book and the 1995 Poetry/Humanities Fair are the result of a collaboration between dozens of poets, teachers and organizations. Special thanks go to those organizations and individuals who helped underwrite this book and its companion anthology, *New Voices in the Humanities*. Among those who contributed were Audrey Geisel, through her Dr. Seuss Foundation; the John R. and Jane F. Adams Endowment; Deborah and Alex Szekeley of the Golden Door and Rancho la Puerta health resorts; and Daniel L. Sullivan, Vice President of Human Resources at Qualcomm Incorporated. Special thanks also go to the poet Joe Milosch, who provided invaluable aid in all aspects of the project; Chris Dickerson of Scripps Ranch High School, whose patience, dedication and moments of inspired brilliance (and just plain common sense) helped everything run smoothly; Sally Owen, who proved a major help (as well as a much-needed expert on punctuation); and the judges who selected the student art and poetry for this anthology: Michelle Esmailian, Greg Dunn of Barnes & Noble, and Rosina Talamantes. A VERY special thanks to *The San Diego Union-Tribune* for agreeing to co-sponsor the project, and to publish student poems, fiction and essays in the newspaper at the time of the fair.

Following is a list of others who have contributed money, in-kind contributions, or moral support to the Border Voices project.

The San Diego Aerospace Museum; the African American Museum of Fine Arts; James Allen; Barnes & Noble/Bookstar; California Poets in the Schools; Centro Cultural de la Raza; Brandon Cesmat; the San Diego Chargers; Veronica Cunningham; Glover Davis, head of the Master of Fine Arts Program in Creative Writing at San Diego State University; Doug Dickerson; Julia Doughty; Danah Fayman; Gloria Foster; Steve Garber; Diana Garcia; Jana Gardner; Mayor Susan Golding of San Diego; Cesar Gonzalez, founding chair of Chicano Studies at Mesa College; Laurie Harker of the *Union-Tribune*, who designed the 1995 Border Voices poster; Gail "minerva" Hawkins; Tamara Johnson; Steve Kowit of Southwestern College; Kris Linblad of the *Union-Tribune*; Elaine Krieger, director of KidzArtz; Sylvia Levinson of the Old Globe Theatre, whose dedication and enthusiasm inspire others; Barbara London of the San Diego State University Foundation; Ann MacDonald; Nicholas Moramarco; Regina Morin; the Museum of Photographic Arts; Johnnierenee Nia Nelson; the entire staff of the Old Globe Theatre, which agreed to let Border Voices use its facilities during the fair; *The Poetry Conspiracy* magazine; Jerry Rife, a photographer for the *Union-Tribune*; the San Diego Guild of Puppetry; the San Diego Padres; the San Diego Symphony; the San Diego Unified School District, with special thanks to Bill Fox, Bill Burrows, and Ellie Dorman; *San Diego Writers' Monthly*; Drew Schlosberg of the *Union-Tribune*'s Newspaper in Education program; Kathleen Shumate; Celia Sigmon; Janice Tolman; Quincy Troupe of UCSD; Chris Vannoy; Jerry Warren, Editor of the *Union-Tribune*; Jean Ellen Wilder; Ellen M. Willenbecher of the San Diego Museum of Art; Mary Williams; Mary Ellen Wilson; Roxanne Young, and Sandra Zane.

The book and the fair were funded in part by a grant from the California Council for the Humanities, a state program of the National Endowment for the Humanities.

Major Poets

AI

was asked for her biography and replied "Why don't you write the bio, but don't forget that I am multiracial from Tucson originally, and I've come a long way, baby." It is a reply that, in its nuances and diction, goes a long way toward introducing the reader to this remarkable poet. Her poetry is both street-smart and traditional, feisty and grave, elegant and rebellious. Her ethnic background is more hyphenated than most (she is a Native-American/African-American poet), and she has won a multitude of awards, including the 1993 Floralia Prize, the 1987 American Book Award and the 1978-79 Pushcart Prize. Her books include *Blackout*, a novel being published by W.W. Norton, as well as numerous collections of poetry, among which are *Greed* (1993), *Fate* (1991), and *Sin* (1986). The following poem was selected from *Fate*.

Reunions with a Ghost

For Jim

The first night God created was too weak;
it fell down on its back,
a woman in a cobalt blue dress.
I was that woman and I didn't die.
I lived for you,
but you don't care. You're drunk again,
turned inward as always.
Nobody has trouble like I do, you tell me,
unzipping your pants

to show me the scar on your thigh,
where the train sliced into you
when you were ten.
You talked about it with wonder and self-contempt,
because you didn't die
and you think you deserved to.
When I kneel to touch it,
you just stand there
with your eyes closed,
your pants and underwear bunched at your ankles.
I slide my hand up your thigh
to the scar and you shiver
and grab me by the hair.
We kiss, we sink to the floor,
but we never touch it,
we just go on and on tumbling through space
like two bits of stardust that shed no light,
until it's finished,
our descent, our falling in place.
We sit up. Nothing's different, nothing.
Is it love, is it friendship
that pins us down,
until we give in,
then rise defeated once more
to reenter the sanctuary of our separate lives?
Sober now, you dress,
then sit watching me
go through the motions of reconstruction —
reddening cheeks, eyeshadowing eyelids,
sticking bobby pins here and there.
We kiss outside
and you walk off, arm in arm with your demon.
So I've come through the ordeal of loving once again,
sane, whole, wise, I think as I watch you,
and when you turn back, I see in your eyes
acceptance, resignation,
certainty that we must collide from time to time.
Yes. Yes, I meant goodbye when I said it.

—Ai

SANDRA ALCOSSER

has written poetry that is "by turns, tender, dark, sensuous . . . a Gary Snyder without Zen or ecological theory . . . We needn't fear for Sandra Alcosser's women; hardly provident, they are gauche and sinister, protesting and unresigned. They move out." This montage of reactions to Alcosser's work from James Tate, Alicia Ostriker and Hilda Raz, in that order, indicates the powerful effect that this prize-winning poet has on her readers. Alcosser's poems have appeared in *The American Poetry Review*, *The New Yorker*, *The Paris Review*, *The Yale Review* and many anthologies, including *Women Poets from Antiquity to Now* (Random House). Her second book of poems, *A Fish to Feed All Hunger*, was selected by James Tate as the Associated Writing Programs Award Series Winner in Poetry. Alcosser was the founder of the Master of Fine Arts Program in Creative Writing at San Diego State University, where she currently serves as a professor of poetry, fiction and feminist poetics.

What Makes
The Grizzlies Dance

June and finally snowpeas
sweeten in the Mission Valley.
High behind the numinous meadows
lady bugs swarm, like huge
lacquered fans from Hong Kong,
like the serrated skirts
of blown poppies,
whole mountains turn red.
And in the blue penstemon
grizzly bears swirl
as they bat snags of color
against their ragged mouths.
Have you never wanted to spin
like that on hairy, leathered
feet, amid the swelling berries
as you tasted a language
of early summer? Shaping
the lazy operatic vowels,
cracking the hard-shelled
consonants like speckled
insects between your teeth,
have you never wanted
to waltz the hills
like a beast?

— Sandra Alcosser

Mayeia Padilla

JUAN FELIPE HERRERA

was born in 1948 in California, the son of farmworkers. His poetry has been published widely in the United States and Latin America, and he's published four books, icluding his first, *Rebozos of Love*, which appeared in 1974, and the award-winning *Facegames* (1987). He received an MFA in Poetry from the Iowa Writers' Workshop, where Iowa scion of poetics Marvin Bell declared that Herrera "goes beyond the sometimes brittle and insular thought-model we are taught to recognize as poetry." Herrera has been active in the performance poetry scene in the San Francisco Bay area, and he has taught extensively both in college and in elementary and high schools. His work has been adapted for the stage and he has been a mural organizer in California, a script writer for the award-winning film *Chicano Park*, an actor for Teatro Campesino and founder of performance troupes. Currently, he teaches in the Chicano and Latin American Studies Department at California State University, Fresno, where he lives with the poet Margarita Luna Robles. The following poem is from *The Roots of a Thousand Embraces* (1994).

Cover(s)

Instructions:

Go ahead, come on — take what's on the top shelf, it's OK
if you buy it, indulge for a day. Now, take the cover off of
each text, be forceful, let the emotions loosen a bit, tear
things off, make casting-out gestures with the arms, let
the face grimace; now — come on — now. Move around a
little and spray your letters on the little page; take the
volumes back to their original places — if you are caught
just say you are simply *re-turning* them.

— Juan Felipe Herrera

FRED MORAMARCO

achieved a notoriety granted few poets when he appeared before a crowd of 40,000 at the home opener of the Padres baseball team on April 4, 1994, and read his poem saluting outfielder/superstar Tony Gwynn. Moramarco's appearance was arranged by the Border Voices Poetry Project as part of an ongoing effort to showcase poetry in San Diego. When not reading his poetry in stadiums filled with sports fans, Moramarco teaches American Literature at San Diego State University; he is also the author of numerous books and scholarly articles, including *Men of Our Time: An Anthology of Male Poetry in Contemporary America* (1992). His poems have appeared in such magazines as *The New York Quarterly*, *Antennae*, *The Pacific Review*, *Paragraph*, *Poetry East* and others. He is currently concluding work on his book *Containing Multitudes: Poetry in the United States Since 1950*. The following poem has not been previously published.

At the Garage Sale

At the garage sale I went to last Saturday,
boxes and boxes of cassette tapes,
the music of their owners' lives,
lay strewn across the sidewalk like blood
splattered from a crime scene.
And there were books, cartons of them,
carrying memories of nights in soft chairs
to the unforgiving asphalt of the street.
There were cups and pots,
whole evenings of lingering meals,
whole 4th of July picnics, thanksgiving dinners
settled in kettles and roasting pans
that now seemed rusted and still,
like the overused grill,
sitting in the corner,
waiting for somebody to offer a buck.

At the garage sale I went to last Saturday,
there were children searching through boxes of yesterday's toys,
mothers sifting through piles of clothing on the porch.
There were artists looking for frames,
teachers looking for classroom games,
beggars needing shoes with full soles,
athletes seeking a well-worn mitt,
and others wanting something to surprise them
in what's left behind by the people who change lives,
who move on in the world
to the next astonishing adventure
that rushes by you like a comet,
unless you stop and stay still, watching
the silent blaze it makes in the sky,
trailing, not only clouds of glory, but of love.

— Fred Moramarco

OJENKE

recites his poetry with a dynamic intensity that has earned him the title of "the John Coltrane of Black Poetry." One of the original members of the Watts Writers Workshop, Ojenke has published extensively in anthologies and magazines, including *The Antioch Review*, *Giant Talk*, *Black World* and *The American Indian Review*. He has published one volume of poetry, *The Mind is a Circular Blade*, from which the following untitled poem was extracted.

Artwork: "The Unknown" / Tom Arthur / Challenger Jr. High

All the stars are the autograph of God

The camel-leopardalia rises triple head and shoulders

above the see-level of men

and peers into the points of light

sprinkled above

Is this love?

to have the band of lights

buckled about the waist

the pure crystal waters falling from above

where one drop of it quenches the thirst

of camel-leopardalia forever

— Ojenke

Hector Amezcua

MARGARITA LUNA ROBLES

is a poet, novelist, short story writer, producer of jazz-poetry con-
certs, and teacher of Chicano-Latin American culture at California
State University, Fresno. Her poems and articles on the poetry scene
have appeared in numerous publications, and she has recited/per-
formed her poetry at venues around the United States, including the
University of Iowa, Stanford University and A Spring for Change
Spring Festival in Santa Cruz, California. She is currently working
on a novel entitled *Identifiable Markings*, based on the murder of a
15-year-old Chicano gay prostitute in Golden Gate Park, San Fran-
cisco. She has published one book of poetry, *Triptych: Dreams,
Lust and Other Performances* (Santa Monica College Press, 1993)
from which the following poem is taken.

Self-Portrait on the Border Between Mexico and the United States (1932)

I can paint myself beautiful in pink
on the border
one foot resting on the past
the other on the future

Mexican sun spills fire
through an angry mouth in a white cloud
the steps of the pyramids wait
a pile of stones formed with wisdom
a forgotten clay Indian god
desert flowers bloom
the dead skull of the past now brittle
the dark cloud embracing a tilted crescent moon
crashing into the sun's sphere, a bolt of lightning
splits the sky

An American dream waves a U.S. flag
over the future
progress
coal mines shooting into the air
the oil will spill
I will slip
lose my balance
fall

And the pink dress will tear and get
dirty.

— Margarita Luna Robles

GARY SNYDER

is one of the giants of American poetry in the second half of the 20th Century. He has published 15 books of poetry and prose, and won the Pulitzer Prize for poetry in 1975 for his book *Turtle Island*. His collection of selected poems, *No Nature*, was a finalist for the National Book Award in 1992, and he is a member of the American Academy of Arts and Letters and the American Academy of Arts and Sciences. Because of his association with such writers as Jack Kerouac, Allen Ginsberg, and Kenneth Rexroth during the great flowering of West Coast poetry that began in the 1950s, Snyder has sometimes been identified with the Beat Generation. But his work is also heavily influenced by his years studying Zen Buddhism at temples and monasteries in Japan, as well as by his love of the natural world, a love that began as a boy on the family farm in the Pacific Northwest. Since 1985 he has been a member of the faculty at the University of California, Davis. The following poem is from his current book-in-progress, *Mountains and Rivers Without End*.

Instructions

Fuel filler cap
  — haven't I seen this before? The
  sunlight under the eaves, mottled
  shadow, on the knurled rim of
  dull silver metal

oil filler cap
  bright yellow, horns
  like a snail — the oil is
  in there — amber, clean, it
  falls back to its pit

oil drain plug
  so short, from in to out. Best
  let it drain when it is hot

engine switch
  off, on, — off, on, — just
  two places. forever,

  or, not even one

      — Gary Snyder

Marina Morrow / Grade 12, Scripps Ranch High

Student
Poets

"Click" / Hillary Cowan / Grade 8, Challenger Jr. High

Enter Here

This door is not just a block of wood
to open or close.
It is not just a passageway
with a handle to grasp.
This door leads east, west,
north and south,
to the light and dark.
A door is not just a picture on hinges.

SARA SCHRELL
Grade 7, Standley Jr. High
Poet-Teacher: Brandon Cesmat
Teacher: Bob Frain

Stars

When I open the door
to the stars
of space
an eclipse
blinded the eyes of
my heart.

CODY TAYLOR
Grade 3, John Adams Elementary
Poet-Teacher: Steve Garber
Teacher: Tamara Hays

Poetry

Poetry is a piece of me
memories, dreams, and thoughts
flying across the paper
Poetry of all colors
like rivers of red, purple, and white
snaking through my thoughts
Poetry is like a burning candle
dying little till the end of the page
Poetry is paper
paper with powerful, meaningful words yelling out
props of emotion
whirling in a poet
making poetry
Poetry is my words
Poetry is my thoughts
Poetry is a piece of me

AYZZA CAMACHO
Grade 7, Standley Jr. High
Poet-Teacher: minerva
Teacher: Margaret Joseph

Box of Feelings

A box from an attic
covered with dust
is a time capsule
filled with secrets,
exploding with colors:

Green
for its envy,
being left behind;

Blue
for its sadness
among the spiders and thoughts;

Red
for the fire of memories
burning its mind,
trapped inside.

There is no edge
without feeling,
no corner
without emotion.

A box means
endless possibilities.

JAMES HENRY
Grade 5, Hawthorne Elementary
Poet-Teacher: Jim Allen
Teacher: Jim Riley

Whispering Words

Why do we have such beautiful things in our world, yet we don't
notice them?
Why is most love shoved away like nothing when it is so beauti-
ful?
Are people born with evil hearts or are they driven to that kind of
life?
How did we become so intelligent when we started out as
cavepeople?
Why do some people have to suffer while others are buying
diamonds and yachts?
Why are each of us so different?
Why do some people possess only love and others only hate?
Why does mankind have such a need for knowledge?
Is there a reason for our existence?

ANNIKA KUBISCHTA
Grade 6, Clear View Elementary
Poet-Teacher: Veronica Cunningham
Teacher: Shiela LeCompte

13 Ways of Looking at a Question

Where does time go after it passes?
What's the other 86 percent of our brain doing?
Does the universe end?
What's beyond it?
What is the middle pedal on a piano for?
Who lit the sun?
Does pain ever suffer?
Why do we kill each other over imaginary lines?
Was geometry created by Satan?
Why is killing a person worse than killing a cow?
Who's the "they" in "that's what they say"?
Why are you a murderer if you kill
one person, a hero if you kill an entire
army of people?
How do we know we're not being brainwashed?

SARAH EGGERS
Grade 10, Point Loma High
Poet-Teacher: Glory Foster
Teacher: Rosemarie Smith

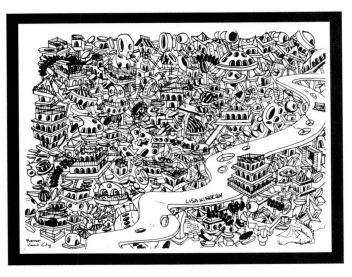

"My House" / Lisa Kingery / Grade 11, Serra High School

The City

The heat rises from the asphalt
in waves and envelopes me.
The chaos of traffic rushes
past me in a cacophony of horns.
I can feel the ground move
under my feet.

The ever-moving crowd of pedestrians
never stops, all faces are unseeing masks.

The steel and mirrored skyscrapers
reach for the horizon
but never quite make it,
while a homeless man in rags
slumps at the door,
a sign of broken dreams.

Children run and shout in the streets
past the graffiti-covered walls,
past the drug dealers on the corner.
I wish they would keep running and never stop.

Night falls, and tiny lights
brighten the skyline,
each one a microcosm
of human life.
In each apartment
there might be a family,
a place remaining among the gaudy neon lights, forgotten dreams,
crime and filth.

JENNIFER KNIERIM
Grade 11, Valhalla High
Poet-Teacher: Joe Milosch
Teacher: Claire Tremaine

The Park

When I was a baby,
my daddy took me to the park
every day.
I would sit in the baby swing
as he pushed me,
and I smiled,
day in, day out.

Then, he took me as a little girl,
taught me how to jump off the swing,
showed me that the slide wasn't scary.
We did somersaults on the grass,
then ate a picnic lunch.
My new baby sister watched
as I played
almost everyday.

When I went to kindergarten,
I played on the monkey bars.
My daddy didn't live with me,
but when he visited,
we went to the park,
played Indians, climbed everything
once a week.

As I grew to eight or nine,
my father took me to museums
or to friends' houses and his apartment,
but sometimes to the park
to swing, to look in the bushes
for colored leaves, pinecones, water, and ladybugs.

Then we moved.
We rode bikes to the park
and roller-skated around,
bought popsicles from the ice cream man,
explored the canyon.
When we visited Dad, we went to the park,
played slide monster and spun crazily
on tire swings,
once a month or less.

Now, we don't go to the park,
except to watch my first grade sister play.
I pass the park on my way home from school.
A few mothers stand with their babies crawling around.
Teenagers in concert shirts head into the canyon
for who knows what reason.
They bully the kids who come to the park from school,
and I see myself in a park, a little tiny girl.

ELISHA COHN
Grade 9, Standley Jr. High
Poet-Teacher: Joe Milosch
Teacher: Marty Baker

Memoirs Upon the Dnieper

A dense fog covers Kiev.
Racing along the highway,
I see a man
at the side of the road,
holding Vodka to trade for gas.
Civilians are not alone, hard-pressed,
jets lay grounded on the air strips.
The tall buildings seem far removed from Chernoble.
The air, however, does not.
I am engulfed by a cloud of nostalgia,
I reminisce of Kiev's Rus,
as Mongolia, Russia lacks its capital.
Madeline Albright demands de-nuclearization.
Too great a threat?
Who are we to tell Leonid Kravchuk
to tell the people of Kiev
about nuclear disaster?

MATTHEW LONGO
Grade 11, Scripps Ranch High
Poet-Teacher: Jim Allen
Teacher: Chris Dickerson

Red Hands

Small boy
twirling on carousel,

slapping his horse,
yelling words he heard in a western.

His hand turns red from slapping
his horse.

His yells become a hoarse laryngitis
that annoys anyone within two meters.

The ride stops.
His mother pulls him off.

He kicks and screams. She slaps him.
He mumbles bad thoughts while
his mother pulls his arm.

PIERRE ORR
Grade 7, Standley Jr. High
Poet-Teacher: Brandon Cesmat
Teacher: Wendy Cobb

Not a Vacant Lot

She crouches on the sidewalk,
staring at all the cars going by.

She wears rags on her shoulders,
rags on her legs.

You watch her.
She murmurs and murmurs
all that she knows.

A tear washes a
streak of dirt from her face.

She cries
remembering her life.

Tears make a mud puddle
around her bare feet.

She stands up and slides her feet over
the sidewalk and down the block.

ELISA HOUGHTELIN
Grade 7, San Pasqual Union
Poet-Teacher: Brandon Cesmat
Teacher: Linda Greenwood

Together

He stands
at the school.

He is sweeping the floor
and cleaning the desktops.

The old red shirt with holes
and blue jeans are dirty.

He talks to himself
so he won't feel lonely.

JOSE ARIAS
Grade 4, Pauma
Poet-Teacher: Brandon Cesmat
Teacher: Catherine Mancino

Grey

The smell of
the metal shavings
burning the grey
grazing lathe is
spinning at 3,500 rpm.
I touch the
insert; it's as
hot as the sun. The sound
of the machine,
louder than a
Greyhound bus.
The cutting oil
sprays in my
mouth. I fall
to the ground
choking; it tastes
like rotting cabbage
sitting outside of
a store for
a week.

I check the
metal device. I
take it out
of the chuck.
My finger scrapes
against the burr
of the insert
and cuts my finger.
The day is
over, and the
machine looks like
it has been to hell and back:
oil on the
chuck, and blood
on the insert.

KADRIJA MAKSUTOVIC
Grade 9, Standley Jr. High
Poet-Teacher: Joe Milosch
Teacher: Rob Larson

"The Window" / Emerald Nazal / Challenger Jr. High

Her Kitchen

The light from the kitchen
flickering on and off.
My mother's shadow dancing playfully on the wall.
She is at the helm of the oven,
which is grumbling and hissing,
dispensing smells beyond imagination.
She battles fiercely with knives and spatulas,
pots and pans, salt and pepper.
I want to offer assistance,
but she pushes me away,
for she knows she's the only captain.

JAMES EDER
Grade 10, Point Loma High
Poet-Teacher: Glory Foster
Teacher: Rosemarie Smith

En la Casa del Mi Abuelita

Al amanecer entraba la luz del sol
al cuarto donde dormía. Al despertar
entrada el olor de tocino con huevos.
Al levantarme, viendo ahí fuera.
De la ventana veía el trafico de los
carros. Oía el canto de los pájaros.
Sentía el calor del sol como un
abrazo de mi papá.

In My Grandma's House

I awoke to rising sunlight
in the room where I slept.
The aroma of bacon and eggs came to me.
I rose from the bed to see outside.
Through the window, I saw the traffic.
I heard the birds sing.
I felt the sun's warmth like a
hug from my father.

ELISA PARRA
Grade 10, Kearny High
Poet-Teacher: Brandon Cesmat
Teacher: Virginia Sánchez-Bernardy

Dad's Beard

Sometimes when I look at my dad's beard
I see little tiny dots all over, and
it makes me think of pepper.
Sometimes it reminds me of fire
because it hangs down and it's all red.
It smells like cigarettes.

BRIANNA CAUSEY
Grade 3, Palomar Mountain
Poet-Teacher: Brandon Cesmat
Teacher: Karen Beck

Thanksgiving

Thanksgiving at my house is like
a thousand bees humming
a peaceful bear sleeping
a pride of hungry lions feasting
little puppies playing
Thanksgiving at my house is like a freeway.

JULIUS MAYO
Grade 6, Fred Baker Elementary
Poet-Teacher: Johnnierenee Nelson
Teacher: Rose Taylor

My Grandma's Kitchen

My grandma's kitchen always smelled good,
never messy, always clean.
There was always something good to eat,
water on the stove, boiling in a rage,
tortillas growing big, ready to explode,
beans bubbling hot with melting cheese.
My grandma would walk in and ask me,
"Are you hungry?" But it's too late.
Me and my sister are already eating.
Today I make breakfast for my grandma.
Now I ask her, "Nana, are you hungry?"

LUCRICIA RODRIGUEZ
Grade 9, Standley Jr. High
Poet-Teacher: Celia Sigmon
Teacher: Norma Fox

The Last Piece of Chicken

The last piece
of chicken on

the chicken bone
that nobody ate

will satisfy a
cat

which will feed
her baby kittens

that lie still
in a pair
of mittens.

CHARLENE SAINT CLAIR
Grade 7, Standley Jr. High
Poet-Teacher: Mary Williams
Teacher: John Sturgeon

HOME

OCTOPUS iN THE DARK
DEPTH OF THE SEA
i'M BLACK, i'M BLUE, i'M RED
SNEAKING ALONG BEYOND MYSELF
GRASPING TO FiND THE END
LiViNG A LiFE iN A SiNGLE DAY
EATiNG MY OWN SOUL FOR FUEL
FOR FUEL, FOR FiRE, FOR LiFE
FOR LiFE iN WHiCH i PARTLY LiVE
FOR LiFE i TRY TO CREATE
FOR LiFE i RUN FROM
FOR LiFE
FOR LiFE
FOR LiFE OF PAiN
PAiN OF LOSiNG LiMBS
WiSHiNG FOR EiGHT
WiSHiNG FOR THiRTY-SEVEN
THiRTY-SEVEN, UNEVEN, iRREGULAR
A BREATH OF CLEAN AiR
iN THE PUNGENT CAGE OF MY LiFE
OF MY DEEP, DARK OCEAN
OF MY HOME
MY HOME, MY SEA, THE PLACE i WiLL LiVE
THE PLACE i WRiTE
THE PLACE i EAT
THE PLACE i BREATHE iTS PUNGENT MASS
THE PLACE MY FiRE BURNS
THE PLACE MY FiRE DiES
FiRE DiES WHERE i AM EXPECTED TO LIVE
HAPPiLY SUBMiSSiVE

DARCY LAMBERT
Grade 8, Standley Jr. High
Poet-Teacher: Glory Foster
Teacher: Sally Owen

49

El Campo y La Ventanilla

Fuera de un pueblo pequeño de un país extranjero,
campos y campos de hierba muerta están durmiendo,
listos para que el aliento de la primavera despierte.
Un granero o casa puede aparecer ocasionalmente,
pareciendo tan extraviado con
pintura astillada y persianas rotas:
Casa, casa dulce.
La iglesia sola
pintado de un blanco inmaculado.
El aliento de Dios en esta tierra,
la fragancia de la cosecha reciente
por la ventanilla bajada
y la paz llena mis pulmones.
Entones, un camión grande pasa
desbaratando la vida de los pocos en las casas
　　　al lado del camino.
Por mi ventanilla
me doy cuenta de la belleza de la vida
fuera del paisaje del pueblo pequeño.
Del otro lado de la ventanilla,
veo belleza.

The Field and the Car Window

In a small town of a distant country,
fields and fields of dead grass lay sleeping,
ready for spring's breath to awaken them.
A barn or ranch house may occasionally appear,
seeming so out of place with
chipped paint and broken shutters:
home sweet home.
The single church painted immaculate white.
God's breath on the land,
the fragrance of the recent harvest
blows through my lowered window
and peace fills my lungs.
Then a large truck passes,
disturbing the life of the few
*   who live in the roadside homes.*
From my window, I sense life's beauty
outside the little town's scene.
From the other side of the window,
I see beauty.

LAVINA RICH
Grade 12, Kearny High
Poet-Teacher: Brandon Cesmat
Teacher: Virginia Sánchez-Bernardy

"The Doves" / Bindi Mundsinghe / Challenger Jr. High

The Doves

Her hands are beautiful
but slightly creased with age,
weathered, and worked to the bone.
Carefully she dresses in her scarf,
quickly folding
and smoothing the scarlet cloth,
perfecting lines and details,
softly stroking the golden strands.
Standing behind her,
I ask her mirror image,
"What time will you be leaving?"
She distractedly answers,
"Yes, but don't stay up too late."

BINDI MUNASINGHE
Grade 8, Challenger Jr. High
Poet-Teacher: Glory Foster
Teacher: Martha Livingston

The Hidden Secret

Clothing, a revolutionary act of mystery.
I wrap myself in material,
uninformed of its significance.
I am taught how to behave, what to wear,
only to liberate myself from these restrictions.

I am enclosed in symbols of my thought,
concealing my emotions.
My attire drips out through a puncture
in my heart.
Like tears pertaining to every soul,
all clothing belongs to mankind.

A rubber band forms a taut barrier.
It stretches, collapses and loosens its hold.
I realize a lighted path.
I shift views and stand apart,
a turquoise gem in the midst of white sand.

SONIA NARANG
Grade 10, Scripps Ranch High
Poet-Teacher: Celia Sigmon
Teacher: Chris Dickerson

My Father's Hands

My father's hands are calloused from years of working on the sea. Now, he works a feather into a squid—a deadly bait. He has been to many exotic places: Africa, Panama, Colombia, chasing the elusive tuna. If I could go back to that time, be back on board that clipper, I would ask my father to teach me the tricks of his trade, the secrets to catching the giant tuna. My father turns with a fish in his hands, and with a questioning look, says, "Your fate is bound to the sea, you were born with the smell and the sound of the sea upon you, and you will die with the smell and the sound of the sea upon you. It is your destiny."

ROB FLETCHER
Grade 10, Point Loma High
Poet-Teacher: Jim Allen
Teacher: Cynthia Hedges

Power Words

She felt as though her heart
would shatter into a million slivers,

as though she had the age-old
soul of a ninety-year-old woman.

Her eyes began to water, and
a river of tears streamed endlessly.

Emotions like ocean currents roughly
swirled around inside.

REINA SORIA
Grade 8, Olive Pierce Middle
Poet-Teacher: Steve Garber
Teacher: Bonnie Ingalls

Brown

So soft, so cool,
just like a cloud,
but not. More like a herd
of funky cows.
When I talk to Brown,
I cover my eyes
with a smile on my face
because she's so cool but funky.

She'll remind you of Woodstock,
a calm chick, brown bell-bottoms
and loud clogs.
Irresistible,
the way the post holds her up.
At this moment,
everything is completely unreal.

Her bouquet
makes her perfume
taste like a box of chocolates,
and her contact is like hot fudge
melting
through my fingers
and before my eyes.

ADRIAN GRAYS
Grade 11, Twain High
Poet-Teacher: Joe Milosch
Teacher: Diane Marshall

Teeth Need Sand

To keep crowds off their pajamas.
chairs grow thorns to keep kids off
since they can't find a sign that says,
"Take One!"
But they found signs that say,
"Beware of Child," and
"Keep Off the Roof."
Teeth hate jerks,
yet notebooks like ice cream cones.
Kids do work while
grown-ups sit down in offices and count scars.
Cardboard hates everybody.
Trees love to have their limbs brushed
while balloons play with needles.
Seedy bushes love jerky
and grassy fields love to play
Terry's and Jerry's new game called "Marshmallow Head."
Schools aren't for learning,
but for parents to have some time alone.
Where will this end?
Why should it?

JORGE JUAREZ
Grade 6, Pauma
Poet-Teacher: Brandon Cesmat
Teacher: Ellen Humphrey

"The Rose" / Mandy Madson and Jessica Risley / Scripps Ranch High

The White Rose

The rose
fresh with tiny water
drops glimmering in the morn-
ing sunlight. Its long majestic
white satin petals unfold as
the sun appears in
the horizon.
The rose's
stem
long
and
strong,
connected
with
numerous
amounts
of long,
deep
roots
like a
river.
The rose, the leader, the queen of mother nature. For
only this rose contains such beauty, elegance,
and grace, like a ballerina.
It is the White rose.

KRISTY ORTIZ
Grade 9, Helix High
Poet-teacher: Jana Gardner
Teacher: Ray Mounts

Masks Abstract

This dying rose
is like my grandmother,
wilting away . . .
yet not quite gone,
warmth
still radiating
from the center
but ready to float away
on the wind.
The endless stairway
winds up into
the deepest peace of mind.
You know
something
someone
has to be there;
you just can't reach it,
winding up the stairs,
but the stairs never
stop winding.
The person
is there
somewhere,
yet hiding,
like a child,
behind the dark,
brittle doorway of petals.

LESLIE CREWS
Grade 8, Standley Jr. High
Poet-Teacher: Glory Foster
Teacher: Sally Owen

The Rose

The rose is like my grandmother
A lady of the past
No thorns left to hurt
Only love
A painting
Old and frail
Pale orange fringed with burgundy
The scent drifting like a ship at sea
But the lady still has
Beauty
Her real self still inside
The sunset is slowly fading
Away

TREZ McBEAN
Grade 8, Standley Jr. High
Poet-Teacher: Glory Foster
Teacher: Sally Owen

The Pencil Sharpener

grinds my pencil
down to the eraser,

sits
and waits
to be fed
a banquet of pencils.

When someone feeds it,
it is a silver horse
being fed a carrot,

swishing its tail
around and around.

LAUREN A. SUSOEFF
Grade 5, Hawthorne Elementary
Poet-Teacher: Jim Allen
Teacher: Jim Riley

The Pencil

lies patient and inconspicuous, carelessly tossed
on a table or in a backpack.

It is worn and battered, and bears the wounds
of long use. The once-new eraser is now a stub.
Its long, yellow backbone is now short
and bears toothmarks.

I imagine a pair of running shoes, muddy and weary
after a hard day's work.

Like a weary soldier, the pencil is content
with a brief respite
from its grueling daily regimen.

KELLY GRIMES
Grade 9, Scripps Ranch High
Poet-Teacher: Jim Allen
Teacher: Brady Kelso

My Hat

My hat
    on my backpack
    is old and ragged
    ripped and stained.

My hat
    is an old man.
It has seen the world.

It knows all secrets.
It appears
    haggard and wrinkled,
    but underneath
    beats a jovial heart.

It has known all I know,
    seen all I have seen.

It is my soul.

MATTHEW OOI
Grade 9, Point Loma High
Poet-Teacher: Jim Allen
Teacher: Cynthia Hedges

Words Cling to Me

My voice is weak, not able to express the inside.
Words cling to me.
It speaks with wanted emotion to express.
Words cling to me.
It sounds deep from within, with a hold-back.
Words cling to me.
I hear emotion around me, yet I have none, but anger and
vengeance.
Words cling to me.
It feels nothing except hot fire from within.
Words cling to me.
It needs emotions I have not.
Words cling to me.
It gives nothing, but anger and no comfort.
Words cling to me.
It fears dark imprisonment of the soul, yet I am there.
Words cling to me.
It would like freedom of the soul.
Words cling to me.
My voice clings to me.

BRIAN BELL
Grade 7, Standley Jr. High
Poet-Teacher: minerva
Teacher: Margaret Joseph

Packed With Peanuts, SNICKERS Really Satisfies

Through the thin paper shield
Concealed in the hard, brown shell
The crunchy, caramel-covered peanuts
The white nougat
The cavity-causing components lie:
Chocolate, Peanuts, Sugar, Salt—
Totaling a fat cal of 120.

Knowing it destroys a woman's fantasy body
Knowing it destroys the Pearl White teeth
Knowing it destroys the desired good health
I take a bite.
Caramel strings stretch for miles
Peanuts make a ruckus in my mouth
It reveals a sweet goodness to my tongue.
Then just as quickly as it came
It went
Taking Satisfaction.

VIENGTHAI PHIMMASONE
Grade 12, Crawford High
Poet-Teacher: Joe Milosch
Teacher: Robin Visconti

My First Day of School

I cried
holding my mom's legs tight.
The teacher came and held my hand.
I cried harder.
Mom said, "I have to leave."
I let go of her legs
and kissed her good-bye.
She watched me as I walked in crying.
I saw a tear drop from her eye
as I turned to say, "Good-bye."
I sat there
sad
lonely
thinking of my mother.

KRISTIN ABORQUI
Grade 7, National City Middle
Poet-Teacher: Roxanne Young
Teacher: Laura Marugg

If I Was Homework

If I was homework,
I would burn for you
and crumple for you and tear
and jump in the fire for you.

GAVIN CARPENTER
Grade 1, Palomar Mountain
Poet-Teacher: Brandon Cesmat
Teacher: Karen Beck

Patient Animals

I stand with my class
waiting to get into the next
animal exhibit.
I hate waiting with knees rattling,
my tongue like a sand dune.
My friends jump up and down
like they have ant farms in their underwear.
My teacher screams the exhibit is clear.
We walk through patiently,
seeing the angry animals
waiting to get out and eat zookeepers.
Outside under the cloud-covered sky,
we go back to school.
How time passes like a bullet train.

JESUS NUÑEZ
Grade 7, San Pasqual Union
Poet-Teacher: Brandon Cesmat
Teacher: Linda Greenwood

Up from the Cellar

The table shakes,
and I begin to shudder.
Muscles tense around my eyes
as a tear manages to escape
like a prisoner climbing from a dungeon or
a deep cellar.
I rattle up and down
like a yo-yo, and
I cling to the rickety table
like it is my shield.

AMY WILLIAMS
Grade 6, San Pasqual Union
Poet-Teacher: Brandon Cesmat
Teacher: Carrie Bronson

My Bus Run

Leaning my face against the bus window,
I feel sweat pour over my face and sting my eyes.
I hear the quiet of the valley.
I smell the feed lots of the dairy.
I see rocks on the mountain sides.
Some trees are jammed with fruit;
others don't have a single orange.
I could taste the juice.
A student hurries out of the academy.
When I get home,
a cool glass of water awaits me.

FREDDIE NUÑEZ
Grade 6, San Pasqual Union
Poet-Teacher: Brandon Cesmat
Teacher: Carrie Bronson

The Lime

My mouth waters like sweat
as I taste it again and again.
It smells like burnt tires on sand,
or like ashes glowing because
they're on fire.
It feels wet, soft,
bumpy and rough.
I rip off a piece.
It looks like a tear,
or a chile pepper.
I touch it with my pencil.
It's dead.
It was alive.
Now that I ate the fruit
it won't move
except when I push it.
The peel looks like a coffin
with one big candle
sticking out,
and flowers all around.

JENNIFER GUTIERREZ
Grade 5, Balboa Elementary
Poet-Teacher: Joe Milosch
Teacher: Terry Cline

The Letter

I have a letter
one written by my father
to me.

It was written on a sad day
in a forbidden room
With an IV in his arm
he wrote the letter to me
with strong scarred hands
that were weak with pain

His hands, left uneven and incomplete
by a thirsty man with a gun

He confessed his love to me
by writing

"I can not wait
to see you
to hold you
and to cry with you."

This, his statement of his love,
is worth more to me than
all the love in the world.

It stays visible in my room
and reminds me of the father
I used to have.

KATHLEEN HALBERG
Grade 11, Valhalla High
Poet-Teacher: Joe Milosch
Teacher: Claire Tremaine

Memories

I remember
my vacations with my family in Mexico
I see
the inside of my grandma's living room
lit by candle light
I remember
our trips on the bus
They took three days
My uncle would pick us up at sunrise
He would always choose me to load our luggage
I felt special
He let us ride in the back of the truck
I remember
arriving
spending time with my grandma
and when my mom finished her cup of coffee
being excused I would run to my Uncle Guillermo's house
to say hi to my three cousins
I would wait
for my uncle to get home
so I could ride his horse
I remember
sitting in his hammock
waiting . . .
losing patience
I would walk to my Uncle Cleofa's house to eat breakfast
and play with my little cousins

Marina Morrow
Grade 12, Scripps Ranch High

I remember
my Aunt Carmen
She sold candy and food
I would get free candy
My cousin Armando would always start some kind of trouble
We would run to my Uncle Auretio's
and my cousin Tito would keep us out of trouble
There we would have lunch
We would take the horse and donkey and leave
I remember
not going to see my two aunts
one would never let me leave and the other had dogs that would bite
I remember
that small village in Nayarit, Mexico
I loved it
Everyone knew me and my bad little ways
I remember my joyous vacations.

LORENZO GARCIA SANDOVAL
Grade 7, Standley Jr. High
Poet-Teacher: Roxanne Young
Teacher: Wendy Cobb

The Mare

I barely came up to her knee.
Her massive hooves could have easily crushed me,
and yet, she wouldn't have hurt a fly.

I had seen this before,
so I was prepared for what was to come.
I backed into the corner.
I stood back . . . and watched.

The six-foot draft horse
writhed in pain on the straw-covered barn floor.
It was humbling to see this majestic animal
in such a state. My uncle approached her warily.

He knelt down, using his elbows to prop himself up on his legs,
those powerful legs that I used to sit on
in the yellow kitchen,
aromas of banana bread curling in my nostrils.

A flash of monstrous, hairy hooves,
and my uncle was on the floor,
grimacing and clutching his gut:
two grand beasts on the ground now.

Foam formed at the corner of her mouth,
a thick, hay-tinted froth that indicated birth was coming soon.
My uncle raised himself to steady the mare,
It's okay girl, yeah pretty girl, it'll be fine.

He stroked her peach-soft nose,
Gary! Pete! GET IN HERE!
It's COMIN'!
and then it came.

Head first—that was unusual.
She's not gonna make it.
The mare's glazed eyes were wide, darting nervously,
a white puss forming in their corners.
An infection.

Okay, we got her.
A knife sliced the life-cord.
We're gonna have to put her down, she won't pull through.
My uncle pulled out his 300 Savage, gleaming black with death.

It was over quickly.
Everything was over.
Exhaustion took over, anticipation was gone,

the uncontrollable thrashing gone, too.
The mare lay lifeless on the barn floor.
It was dispiriting, almost crushing.

Memories flooded my head,
leaking out of my eyes
and dropping on the dry hay.

Days I would spend,
sitting in tall grass that almost covered me,
watching her pull the plow,
her stalwart body
toiling tirelessly,

living life as a towering animal
demanding respect, admiration, and love;
then, leaving this life as a wriggling mass
of hair matted with blood, hay,

and leaving behind a bow-legged, jittery colt.

IVONNE THOMPSON
Grade 10, Scripps Ranch High
Poet-Teacher: Joe Milosch
Teacher: Chris Dickerson

Sun in Florence

I have never seen your hands,
but I have felt their touch.
Your smooth script unfolds across a page
like a warm blanket on a child grown cold.
I wrap myself in the words.

It has been four summers since I have seen the sun in Florence.
The heat coursed through stone streets
and up radiant colonnades,
turning them to gold.
Jagged edges softened as liquid eyes moved towards the center,
the cathedral,
strung on an organ's cedared perfume.
Four years since I longed, unabashed, to lie
in the faded satin of the
domed hope chest,
and watch every note slide against the rounded walls.

An aria of color rained beyond stained glass
as ebbing sun shifted white embers
and you turned to approach me.

Now you write letters
peppered with questions of my world.
Do you want to see the jagged edges?

Gnawed with unsettled hunger,
I draw your words from their cedared chest.
I am moved to pull away the heavy lid
and reveal a spiral of webbed fingers.
Notes from a forgotten score,
left to lull and resound in buried folds
as wild aster,
gasping beneath the leaden cloak of the moor,
longing to lie in the sun.

You were shrouded in the light of a cathedral, and I did not know you.
But as the glove unravels, I see the tense muscles of our palms.
And I cannot let you go, your grasp is so strong.

LAURA BRENNEMAN
Grade 11, Scripps Ranch High
Poet-Teacher: Jim Allen
Teacher: Chris Dickerson

The Coral Reef

This coral reef is like my brother John
his outer body
hard
calloused
unrefined
from years of pounding surf
surf made up of insults and mockery
but if he were broken apart
his heart and soul would appear
full of hidden, unknown microscopic life
and hope
a mirror of his personality
the coral reflects a pleasant, creamy look
but look just a little deeper
and the blackness soon begins to emerge
the broken edges
razor sharp from the experiences
which cut at the body
and the soul
he is tossed
shattered
battered
his shape malformed
like a body seen reflected on a carnival mirror
his inner core
with all its safeguards and barriers
protects him from the outside world
and from the demons within.

BRIAN POLMEAR
Grade 12, Samuel F.B. Morse High
Poet Teacher: Glory Foster
Teacher: Robert Lunsford

What It's Not

The white soap sits
in a soap dish in my bathroom.
Easily it slips through my fingers
just like this poem slips through my mind.
The sudsy little bubbles remind me of my emotions:
transparent and delicate, they are easily broken.
One by one they disappear from view,
and I feel the pain coming.

My hands come up to my face,
washing the tears off my cheeks.
I'm not crying because I'll miss you,
                although I will.
I'm not crying because I love you,
                although it's true.
I am crying because I'm sorry.

It's all in the past now that I know.
But I can't help it.
You forgave me without the explanation you deserved.
I didn't mean to hurt you.
I didn't want to make you cry;
I just wanted you
to love me.

EMILY BOOST
Grade 8, San Pasqual Union
Poet-Teacher: Brandon Cesmat
Teacher: Bryce Bacher

When I Wrote Your Name

When I wrote your name on
    my window
The sun came
    and dried it
    away
When I wrote your name in
    the sand
A wave came
    and washed it
    away
When I wrote your name on
    paper
The teacher came
    and threw it
    away
When I wrote your name in
    my heart
Someone came
    and took it
    away

QUIANA LONG
Grade 8, Olive Pierce Middle
Poet-Teacher: Steve Garber
Teacher: Julie Petry

A Tree for Mom

If I were a tree green and brown,
I would show my love by letting her
make hats of my leaves.
She could climb my trunk
and eat my apples,
sleep in my shade.

MIRIAM ARMSTRONG
Grade 5, San Pasqual Union
Poet-Teacher: Brandon Cesmat
Teacher: Patricia Matson

Don't Cry Over Spilled Blackberries

All the blackberries spilt off the
cloud, pouring forever. Many people
are happy they aren't hungry
any more. They begin to lick up the
juice; a mother begins to feed her
baby; the baby's voice squeals with
delight; the world is happy—and yet
there is sadness: not down below
but up above. It's crying because
it dropped the blackberries.

MICHAEL A. BICKETT
Grade 8, Keiller Middle
Poet Teacher: Mary Williams
Teacher: Oscar Browne

Well, Child

Well, child, I'll tell ya
Life for me ain't been no
nice glass of wine.
It's had poison in it
and dirt
and glass all broken up,
and places with no light
in the house—
dark.
But all the time,
I've been a' drinkin' on
and overcomin' problems
and still climbin' higher
and sometimes goin' in the cold
where there ain't been nothing' for my back.
But I tell you, child, don't turn back.
Don't stop drinkin' your wine
'Cause you'll always find it's kinda hard.
Don't you fall back now—
for you see me, I'se still goin',
I'se still overcomin' problems,
and life for me ain't been no
nice glass of wine.

VELAMA McGHEE
Grade 8, Keiller Middle
Poet-Teacher: Mary Williams
Teacher: Oscar Browne

Watermelon Won't Know

The watermelon rolled through the crowd's legs.
Watermelon has no idea of the differences in these people's
lives,
doesn't know the hard finger tips, cuts and long mornings,
can't imagine the tired muscles of these people waiting.
The watermelon is not aware of a single guy flirting with attached
women,
won't know the greed of the man who just stole a purse,
has no idea of the grief in the woman whose hamster just died.
The elevator opens. People rush to get in.
Spiked heels, sneakers, boots now wet with
watermelon juice.

RACHELLE MANZANO
Grade 8, Standley Jr. High
Poet-Teacher: Brandon Cesmat
Teacher: Jim Harris

My Uncle,
My Aunt and I

My uncle lies dead in his coffin
with nobody at his funeral.

I was the only one there
with my aunt.

I sat on my aunt's lap,
Crying.

ANA MANRIQUEZ
Grade 4, Pauma
Poet-Teacher: Brandon Cesmat
Teacher: Catherine Mancino

Racing

Speed of light racing nowhere . . .
. . . chasing air, too fast for wind to catch.

A long rope of transparent
color.

Smell of silver.
on its way through time.

How fast am I going?
Will I ever stop?
How far have I traveled?

. . . Disappearing in the distance

STEPHANIE CASAO
Grade 5, Highland Ranch Elementary
Poet-Teacher : Jana Gardner
Teacher: Rick Flanders

Holster

This particular holster
was a usual type,
made of hard brown leather
held together by clips and rope.

When you look at it long enough,
it looks like
a little slipper
that a dwarf would wear.

It would have a toe point,
would be soft on the inside.
The bottom would be
hard and tough.

I used to have slippers like those.
They were blue
with beads on them.
They were a present from Turkey.

ANA KODZICH
Grade 9, Standley Jr. High
Poet-Teacher: Joe Milosch
Teacher: Marty Baker

Marina Morrow / Grade 12, Scripps Ranch High

Who Am I?

I am:
King like a lion
hot like summer
scary like Halloween
black and mean.

Strong as a hurricane
loud as a drum
sneaky as a spider
with a circular tongue.

Wild as a car crash
smart as a whip
and when I play football
I never trip.

Wise as an oak tree
helpful like a rainforest—
even though I can't stand
my Auntie Doris.

Mysterious as a black hole
fast as a Ferrari
sweet like candy
and I never say "gnarly."

Gross as a fly-trap
cunning as a zookeeper
not afraid of nothin'
and I never get caught cussin'.

I listen to rap
love to collect hats
eat lots of soul food as
well as shrimp fried cats.

The best thing about me
is really neat, you see.
No one in this whole world
can ever beat me!

D'ANGELO
OVERSTREET
Grade 8, Keiller Middle
Poet-Teacher: Mary Williams
Teacher: Oscar Browne

I Am . . . What?

I am fourteen whispers heard on a
Sunday morning.
I am deer that are
hiding in the burgundy forest,
hoping that the
vicious hunter will go away.
I am a cylinder with
extraordinary dimensions
just waiting to be calculated
by the stressed mathematician.
I am a young poet
pretending to be
things that I will
never be able
to become in this
lifetime.

EMERALD NAZAL
Grade 8, Challenger Jr. High
Poet-Teacher: Glory Foster
Teacher: Martha Livingston

I'm More Than A Nomad

They call me a navy brat
I'm more than a nomad
With my metal smile
    And shoulder length hair.
I'm more than a nomad
I'm as sweet as a lemon
    And as sour as a peach
I'm more than a nomad
I'm as shy as an exhibitionist
    And as aggressive as a mouse
I'm more than a nomad
Home is where your heart is
    And 10 moves prove that
I'm more than a nomad

LAUREN KITCHEN
Grade 8, Challenger Jr. High
Poet-Teacher: Glory Foster
Teacher: Martha Livingston

I Am an Electric Fog

I am an electrical fog
In a circle of excitement
Dare-to-die surfer
Sandy pansy summer
Blue rock be-bop
Sitting on a tree top
Cherry mushroom legend
One-of-a-kind hawk
Wild New Year's party
Crashing thunder hot guitar
Whistle clean jolly
In a crystal wonderland
Romantic fairy-tale
Carrot wood single tree
Bavarian Alps, Germany
Snow-boarding fool
Zipper Bug Dragonfly buzz
Cherry lip kiss
Unicorn Peace Pasture
Living life to its fullest.

LISA STOEFEN
Grade 8, Challenger Jr. High
Poet-Teacher: Glory Foster
Teacher: Martha Livingston

"Water Music" / Kelly Hoyer / Grade 10, Point Loma High School

Music

BAM!   BAM!   bib- BAM!   dah boo-boo bah BEEP!
The beat bashes against my head,
stinging my ears, a bomb by my temples,
from soft and sweet to static with sweat.

Ding-Dong!   chinch- chinch   Crash!

The beat dies down, the brass warms up,
the reeds swell, and the percussion goes wild!

Bee ba da doo   BAH!

With Fingers at the piano, Electric Mojo on the brass,
Tommie the Trigger on the trumpet, Eli on the sax,
Slick on the bone, Vinne on the ge-tar,
and Sticks on the skins, they play
silence shouting, chaos created
the dark sheltered basements their home.

Dum-Bum Bang!   Bang!   reallibang   WHAP!

From the 60s to the 90s, the 20s to the 50s,
the 1700s to the 1900s, The beginning to the end.
repeating, changing, evolving, turning,
whizzing by people, keeping them awake.
Nothing can stop the soul's voice,
the bluebird's song, the meaning of life.

Bah-ba dum dah Bah!   ding-ding-ding CHA!

RICHARD POWELL
Grade 11, Valhalla High
Poet-Teacher: Joe Milosch
Teacher: Claire Tremaine

Singer

He slouches in a chair
guitar on his knees.

His knees touch lightly
against the microphone stand.

Ragged clothes worn for three shows
move slightly as he strikes an A Major chord.

He sings
the song fills the building,
fills the listeners ears,
slightly off key.
They do not notice but
rock and smile.

They do not see
the pain in his eyes or
hear the pain from a hard life,
hard like the fretboard of the guitar
that he carries with him everywhere.

Still he sings, and
they listen.

DANIEL REED
Grade 8, San Pasqual Union
Poet-Teacher: Brandon Cesmat
Teacher: Bryce Bacher

My Life and My Wave

My life is like waves.
It slams against rocks,
yet sometimes it drifts over the sand
with the tide.
Sometimes it rolls rough,
and other times it sits smooth.
Waves are mysterious,
and so am I.
Waves can be cruel and break through windows,
or smooth.
A wave goes many places
and gets through small places in rocks
because it will always fight for what it believes.
I am like the sea
because I make up my mind and
fight rocks for what I believe.

ASHLEY McNERNEY
Grade 5, Pacific Beach Elementary
Poet-Teacher: Brandon Cesmat
Teacher: Adilia Lavado

The Devil
Can Cite Scripture . . .

You say that Jesus loves me
    you in your luxury BMW
    you in your fashionable designer clothes
    you in your superficial mask to conceal
What sort of chasm is your conscience?

You say that Jesus loves me
    you, cutting me off on the freeway
    hindering me without a conscious thought
    no compensation for your inconsiderate action
    your insolence dances to an aristocratic rhythm
What gives you this special privilege?

You say that Jesus loves me
    you and your pathetic attempts at virtue
    reveling at those less fortunate
    constantly puncturing the human spirit
    as a monument of your superiority
Why does your cross burn through your chest?

You say that Jesus loves me
    and you wallow in your privilege
    and you trample and decimate the social jungle
    and you champion 187 degrees of prejudice
    and you circumvent that which morality dictates
What beyond money gives you such rights?

You say that Jesus loves me
　　yet you constantly ignore me
　　and you sneer at my convictions
　　and you choke me with disdain
　　and all you have to offer me is sympathy
Is not yours the most blatant of hypocrisies?

You say that Jesus loves me
　　and you turn to me and scowl
　　your empty eyes look down on me
　　across an acrid ocean of materialism
　　a bitter sigh and then your inquiry
" What is the problem with society?"

JASON MAC GURN
Grade 11, Valhalla High
Poet-Teacher: Joe Milosch
Teacher: Claire Tremaine

"Sunset" / Laika Stepanoff / Challenger Jr. High

I Am

I am the splashing of waves
an endless sea
light reflecting
labyrinth
lost, searching
diving
through this
strange mystic mind
pain never ceasing
love, twisting, turning
binding me
last drop of blood
rushing tears
insane confusion
crazy
sarcastic words
life death
confusing thoughts
I am everything that is
and ever will be
a soul breaking free

JOY FRYE
Grade 9, Helix High
Poet-Teacher: Jana Gardner
Teacher: Jessica Patton

Mandala

My mother loves the beach much more than I do;
she hems the tide with footprint stitches
carelessly unraveling behind.
She goes at night; *ella vea la luna y las olas*
she goes alone.

I've been told there is someone for everyone.
My mother tells me.
The fist that clenches my heart
tightens in rage at her words.
She has found True Love.
That's why she walks alone at the beach?
I shut my eyes.

A hasty note:
"I'm at the beach—Love."
I turn away, the note drifts lightly to the floor.
I see my mother with the moon and sea,
her head turned toward the waves—
she does not plan her next stitch.
This is her reverence, her peace.
This is not her solitude.

MARINA MORROW
Grade 12, Scripps Ranch High
Poet-Teacher: Joe Milosch
Teacher: Chris Dickerson

Marina Morrow
Grade 12, Scripps Ranch High

The Mind's Eye

My mind's eye
sees an ocean ahead of me,
a warm haven
    from the cold and unforgiving sight
    of my ice-clad home.
I can hear the waves crashing,
daring me to wander into their arcing crests,
    away from the silence
    that holds the frozen world
    I will awaken to.
I'll go into warm ocean water,
through the soft snow wave layers,
    and escape my frozen prison, get
    away from my cold nightmares,
    like going to sleep and never waking up.
The water tastes pleasant
as it flows through me,
    unlike ice,
    which must be broken
    before you can eat it, allow it to scar your throat.
Lying back in the sand, the air smells sweet
as the warm sun slowly dries me off.
    My conscious home holds no smell,
    and nothing ever melts.

KIEF ZANGARO
Grade 12, Scripps Ranch High
Poet-Teacher: Joe Milosch
Teacher: Chris Dickerson

Seeing Red

A Found Poem from The San Diego Union-Tribune

As the sky darkens and its colors deepen
The sight will become even more impressive
Clutching her rosary beads
And manipulating the red cellophane flames
Kicking and screaming
Whimpering and whining
I last saw the graceful dance rituals
The forgotten lessons
The controlling flow
While running a mean stretch of rapids
Cavorting through a percussive number
Like human drums
Their bodies covered with coconut shells
Or a pair
Shinnying up poles
Where they spin above the crowd
Or roostering and roistering
In mating competition
Like birds in a cockfight
Nothing can adequately portray
The beauty of the sight.

EMILY S. ERPELO
Grade 12, Samuel F.B. Morse High
Poet-Teacher: Glory Foster
Teacher: Robert Lunsford

Purple's Music

Purple's soft music,
the sway of the color.
    Trembling purple petals,
    touched by the light breeze.
        A careful purple rain,
        sprinkling overhead.

A sea of colorful fish,
purple glimmering in the sunshine.
    A shell so untouched,
    the refreshing sound
    of the ocean hollow.
        The color purple taste
        of a popsicle, melting in the heat.

Perfumey smell
and delicate touch of soft, purple flowers.
    All dancing to the sound of the soft, purple music;
    a gentle violin sways to remember.

RENEE YARMY
Grade 9, Helix High
Poet-Teacher: Jana Gardner
Teacher: Ray Mounts

I Am

I am a candy plum

        secludedly sitting,

a blue cat *zipping by.*

        A STORMY DAY OF *UNPREDICTABLE*

FLASHES.

    I am the pink willow rippling in the *wind.*

A sedate little cottage with the

stout peppery gardenia blooming,

a sultry family room in a house of bitter cold.

A song of a bird gaily caroling heavenly music.

My story never ending,

        and my petite little car keeps . . . putting

along.

CARISSA BREWER
Grade 7, Emerald Middle
Poet-Teacher: Jana Gardner
Teacher: Gail Charles

Sand Shark

As I kick back
in the nice cool sand
at the bottom of the ocean,
I look at everything
above me and wonder
when
my lunch will swim by.

I feel good because
nothing can see me
or spy on me.
I feel like a guard
of the sea
watching everything,
and nobody
even knows
I'm here.

All of a sudden
a good-sized mackerel
swims by.
I go after it
showing my teeth
and not giving him any time
to die or to move.
I swallow him whole.

ARTURO RODRIQUEZ III
Grade 5, Balboa Elementary
Poet-Teacher: Joe Milosch
Teacher: Terry Klein

If I Were a Kitten

I'd be black and white.
I'd hide in your mitten
and stay up all night.
I'd be as big as your hand,
and when you tried to stand,
I'd fall down.

I'd live in your house.
My friend would be a mouse,
and all day I would play and play.

I'd leap through the air
and play with your hair
and give you a scare.

I'd sleep with you at night
and snuggle up tight.
If you tried to snore,
I'd put up a fight.

My eyes would glitter like diamonds.
My coat would be black as coal.
I'd keep as close to you
as a mother horse to her foal.

I'd play baseball with you
even though I couldn't catch,
and I'd never, never
ever, ever scratch.

And you'll just love me,
all these things I'll do.
I'd be your cat of curiosity,
your cat of peace, too.

JESSICA HEALY
Grade 5, Pacific Beach Elementary
Poet-Teacher: Brandon Cesmat
Teacher: Lauri Pierik

"Two Snakes" / Annely Bartolome / Challenger Jr. High

Adventure Through a Stream

As i walk through a field of violet
bees, i spy a stone of wonders
in front of a
delicate
stream.
As i sail over the stone
of wonders and plunge in
the delicate stream, it cries out in
pain as piercing as the snoring catfish jewel.
As i adventure through the stream,
i find a fragile goldfish that
marks
the place of everlasting deep
waters, as drowning as the plain,
or bitter mouse's squeak. i go as brave as
the Tyrannosaurus, maroon-
spotted as night, into
the dauntless, gloomy waters. i
smell the giant manatee, turning
back, furiously grey as a
tarnished blue diamond. i plunge
out, gilded with the wings of
galaxies. i whisk through the sweet
smelling bluebell daisies of
pines. i skip with the black-haired
stars
of
night, through the
field of violet bees, the
sunset, ruffling my turquoise
hair that's lime green as the
prehistoric cheese moon.
i go swiftly home as the
maroon-dotted sun sets on
my
adventure   ELISA ASHLEY CRAWFORD
through   Grade 3, Highland Ranch Elementary
a   Poet-Teacher: Jana Gardner
stream.   Teacher: Joanie Hedstrom

A Leaf Through the Seasons

The snow melts
Down the mountain
The river flows
A tree sits bare
The sun shines through the clouds
A leaf starts to grow
I am a leaf
I am small, it is spring
I feel raindrops, now sunlight
Summer, it is warmer
The rain doesn't fall much anymore
Autumn, the clouds come back, it is cooler
I am changing, the wind blows, it is cold
I turn yellow and orange
I turn light brown
I am dry and crumbly
I feel weak
The harsh wind blows, I break free
Falling to the ground
I see large trees with pointy leaves
They are green
I am buried in snow
It is winter

MICHAEL HEAD
Grade 6, Lindbergh/Schweitzer Elementary
Poet-Teacher: Roxanne Young
Teacher: Lisa Lee

I Am a Bright Shooting Star

I am a bright shooting star slowly moving
across the sky.
I am a bright shouting star reaching everyone's
heart.
I am a bright shooting star. I am red, yellow, peach
and silver.
I shoot to the lovely planets.
I shout to the universe.

DAVID SONG
Grade 6, Lindbergh/Schweitzer Elementary
Poet-Teacher: Roxanne Young
Teacher: Lisa Lee

El Arbol del Familia

Hay un árbol fuera de la ventana.
Las flores lentamente se mueven con el viento
en las ramas delicadas del árbol.
El árbol es una famila junta pero separada.
Cada rama crece en diferentes direcciones
pero no puede crecer fuera del árbol
compartiendo la misma conexión
pero nunca encontrando la dirección apta.
Es un árbol de amor e indiferencia.
Este es el árbol de familia.

Family Tree

There is a tree outside the window.
Flowers slowly move with the wind
on the tree's delicate branches.
The tree is a family separated together.
Each limb grows in a different direction
but cannot outgrow the tree.
Beginning with the same roots
but never coming together as they should
is a tree of love and indifference.
This is the family tree.

CHRISTIE LOVE
Grade 11, Kearny High
Poet-Teacher: Brandon Cesmat
Teacher: Virginia Sánchez-Bernardy

Seeing My Sister

Every day my little sister would climb the tree by our house.
She could climb like a monkey without falling,
as fast as a lizard.
Her clothes were tight blue shorts,
big T-shirts and white high-tops.
She would climb into her room from the branches
and turn the radio
as high as she could, and dance.
Her room had the smell of roses.
On her light-brown dresser,
she had a crystal-clear bear and
a lot of stuffed animals.
She would climb that tree every day after school.
But now that she's gone,
I don't know what she does.
The walls are closing,
her dolls looking at me.

MAURISA LaCHUSA
Grade 6, Pauma
Poet-Teacher: Brandon Cesmat
Teacher: Ellen Humphrey

If I Were a Tree

I
Would
Cover Earth
With My Breath.
Spend The Day Dancing,
In The Golden Sun.
The Sparkling Rain Would Cleanse
My Evergreen Branches,
Catching The Rain, Falling Crystals Of Life.
I Would Reach Out,
And Touch A Dancing Rainbow.
The Shiny Moon Would Scare Me, Tossing Branches,
With Fright.
The Fiery Sun Comes Up, And The Birds Which Live Within
Wake Me, With The Dawn.
I Would Be
The Center
Of Existence
To The World
That Stood
Below.

JOANNA BERRY
Grade 8, Olive Pierce Middle
Poet-Teacher: Steve Garber
Teacher: Connie Mendoza

Moon Shell

Where did the moon shell come from
landing on the sea of jade emerald,
washing upon the dove-white shore
of dainty roses,
dancing its way to stars of lilies, and
glistening against the glowing moon of morning dew?

In the daytime, it poured along with rain of the
purest diamonds
mixed along with bricks of ruby
sailed in the sky of sapphire
into the blaze of copper-gold
into the cave of dim silver.

Then it went into the sky again during the night of
coal
back to the moon of morning dew, caught on a delicate
shimmering spiderweb,
and nobody knew it was a
pearl of the finest rainbow.

TIFFANY LING TSE
Grade 5, Spreckels Elementary
Poet-Teacher: Jana Gardner
Teacher: Janet Posen

Green

Green, what a beautiful color,
a color that I don't like,
as if it held the taste of peas,
brussel sprouts, green beans
or lettuce.
It smells like pines, fresh cut grass, green apples, avocado
and spices.

The sight of trees, leaves, grass,
clothes and animals.
It feels like the touch of seaweed, slime, crayon, toys or chalk-
boards.
I wish I could think of green and hear crickets,
trees rustling in the wind,
and someone's green shoes squeaking.

MELISSA BRADFORD
Grade 9, Twain High
Poet-Teacher: Joe Milosch
Teacher: Diane Marshall

Haunting Green

Green is the endless meadow
in the dawn of a new day.

You are the color
of my silky soft sweater.

You are the green feather
that floats to the ground
from a bird
passing overhead.

Why are you such
a haunting color?

You appear everywhere—
the stem of a delicate rose,
the eyes of my defenseless
black kitten.

Where did you come from?

DANIELLE ARZAGA
Grade 5, Hawthorne Elementary
Poet-Teacher: Jim Allen
Teacher: Jim Riley

I Used to . . . But Now

I used to walk through a magical
doorway inside a rainbow of roses,
daisies, violets, marigolds, and chrysanthemums.
I could see mountains of
music, trees of moonlight, animals
of stars, and flowers of sunlight.
I would jump so high I could reach
the silver moonbirds that never
stop flying and play with the
stars. It was beautiful then, when
daytime shone upon the earth,
but now it is night, night,
night.

ALEX STROMBERGER
Grade 4, Highland Ranch Elementary
Poet-Teacher: Jana Gardner
Teacher: Linda Rasmussen

Chimes

Chimes in a big room.
They throw colors on the wall:
blue, silver, purple, pink, black.
My wind chimes are like spoons
clinging together in their places,
like me when I lean over
to whisper to someone.
They are diamonds of gentleness,
shining colors all over the room,
reflecting designs softly
like feathers on the wall.

MELINDA SNAPP
Grade 4, San Pasqual Union
Poet-Teacher: Brandon Cesmat
Teacher: Karalee Gorham

River Poem

In my river I see my mother
working hard for my brother and me,
I hear her soft voice calling my name.
My river is full of love and tenderness,
but also hardships and sadness.
In my river I love to play with my friends,
be with my family, and talk with my mom.
In my river I am the soft petal
of a rose full of dew.
My river begins
in the little town of Mexicali.

ROCIO AHEDO
Grade 7, National City Middle
Poet-Teacher: Roxanne Young
Teacher: Laura Marugg

I Wish

i wish i could skip into the sky with the
moon and stars waiting to greet me
i wish i could swim in a lake of my tears to bring
me up when i am down
i wish i could scream my purple screams till someone
hears my soft whisper
i wish i could leap so high that everything would
            FREEZE!
and acknowledge me

YVE LARIS COHEN
Grade 3, Miramar Ranch Elementary
Poet-Teacher: Jana Gardner
Teacher: Jan Rosell

Us

A cold dark night
two people lie
sweet smoke
fills the air
the fire roars
the candles are low
they've been burning all night
you can still smell the fragrance of black love
her favorite incense
his strong calloused hands
gently grip
her soft smooth shoulders
silence
there is no place they'd rather be
than there
asleep
with each other

CECILE RUBENSTEIN
Grade 12, Monte Vista High
Poet-Teacher: Roxanne Young
Teacher: Carol Pyle

Antler

A crooked crippled piece of bone
knotted by age,
it looks like an egret
standing in a swamp ready to fly.

As you look at it,
when you feel the tip,
you can visualize the figure and form
of its head and curved spine.

An egret is this
which has great wings to fly;
its soft feathers are smooth
and its stalky legs hard and bony.

In the quiet of the dusk
it slowly hunts the fish,
one foot up, one foot down,
silent, careful - SNAP

The egret lives life
taking each day in stride,
a recollection of sights seen.

The antler old and worn
is just a memory of what was,
a relic to the young.

The egret grown old,
a dry parched horn,
the age of old holds my future,
my feebleness, my end.

ANGELA CAMPOS
Grade 9, Standley Jr. High
Poet-Teacher: Joe Milosch
Teacher: Marty Baker

Within Me

There is a deer in me,
a dancing, golden-brown deer.
She prances without a sound
in the leafy green forest.
When I feel her stand, I am peaceful.
When she looks and listens,
I am quiet and calm.
She follows a path the color of fog.

There is a horse in me, too,
a dark brown horse
that never whinnies.
She walks slowly. Sometimes she trots
or gallops.
I am fond of her.
I feel excited that she will take me for a ride.

DIVYA BHATT
Grade 4, San Diego Community Home Education
Poet-Teacher: Brandon Cesmat
Teacher: Linda Gross

The Jumping Frog

My heart jumps
like a frog
My heart jumps with me
like a frog
It is fun jumping
with my heart
With my heart, me and my heart
are jumping
like a frog

CARLOS BAENA
Grade 3, John Adams Elementary
Poet-Teacher: Steve Garber
Teacher: Tamara Hays

Yellow

Yellow,
The soft breeze blowing
a leaf that is an autumn
gold, falling to the ground
softly, even softer than
snow.

Yellow,
The hot sun that is on
my back, while it is
reflecting off my
helmet and making a
trickle of sweat come
down from my head.

Yellow,
The breeze that refreshes
me and helps me go on.

Yellow,
The classical music to
my ears that puts me
to sleep.

EDWIN GARCIA
Grade 9, Helix High
Poet-Teacher: Jana Gardner
Teacher: Ray Mounts

Jaguar

My heart is like a
    jaguar running fast
    as it can
    in the magic cave
    of blue wonder.

MELINDA MONTAG
Grade 5, John Adams Elementary
Poet-Teacher: Steve Garber
Teacher: Edna Felgreber

I'm a Gray, Leaping Dolphin

I'm a gray, leaping dolphin
splashing playfully
daydreaming lifelessly
A slick and sleek pyramid of life
skimming across the sphere of water
blindly devouring fish
The fiery blue water around me
full of explosive energy
reaches for the sky
vegetating wildly on
a lazy Saturday afternoon.

ALVIN POON
Grade 8, Standley Jr. High
Poet-Teacher: Glory Foster
Teacher: Sally Owen

Me

I am a forest-green tiger with pigtails
and black nail polish.

I eat orange kiwis in blue spaghetti
with red watermelon bananas.

I drink wintergreen water that has a
twist of lemon incense.

I play in chocolate snow-covered daisy
fields with musical cantaloupes and
moody dinosaurs.

I wear my sunflower Carebear
Mickey Mouse hat when I fly my
fluorescent Dorrito kite.

I leave strawberry footprints behind
along with blue softballs and
rainbow shoelaces.

DANA IVERSON
Grade 8, Standley Jr. High
Poet-Teacher: Glory Foster
Teacher: Sally Owen

Savior

Plains, hills, canyons, slopes—
streams sliding over sediment,
streams stirring particles of light,
streams crossing over waves.
Boulders lean into, far into
the rush of liquid;
moss bathes in the spray,
clinging to the roots
of a shingled trunk
which wears sunburned leaves
which casts a stretched shadow
which provides shade
for roots, rocks, river.
Grains of sand slowly roll down the slope,
into cracks and crevices
defined by absence of light,
knocking larger grains that tumble down,
skinning the pale surface
around hanging vines
that paint the cliffs with violet brushes.
Wind catches this dry run,
lifting dust in the air,
along with the smell of sage
among the fallen palm leaves.
The heartbeat—
breezes rustling the leaves,
sand scraping the cliff,
water bubbling among the rocks—
is a savior's sound for the few
surviving in the dry wash below.

MICHAEL ASAKAWA
Grade 12, Scripps Ranch High
Poet-Teacher: Joe Milosch
Teacher: Chris Dickerson

Marble Paths

If I were the moon
I would walk across
    a path
of black velvet
    shine
the beacon of heaven
cast white light
    over

shimmering blades
of grass
glittering
with dew
on stormy nights
a cloak of clouds
wraps around me
protecting
my delicate pale beauty.

If I were the moon
I would play cards
with stars
to pass time
I would make coyotes
howl
wildly wanting
to join me
in my elevated kingdom
sing to mountains
in harmony with crickets
spill
over the sea
like marble paths.

ELYSIA JENNETT
Grade 8, Olive Pierce Middle
Poet-Teacher: Steve Garber
Teacher: Connie Mendoza

The Bald Eagle

So great and massive in the sky am I
Leaf floating from a tree to the ground
Stone made from dirt and gold
A plane, but no pilot
A spirit, but you can see me
Soaring higher than clouds
Bold and beautiful is the gold
Dark and wonderful is the brown
Twirl around twice as you fly with me
You're welcome to eternity
So great and massive in the sky am I

STEVEN NGUYEN
Grade 4, Miramar Ranch Elementary
Poet-Teacher: Jana Gardner
Teacher: Pam West

The Language of the World

Are child, serpent, star and stone all one?
What happens before life?
Why does the fancy rat hide inside your shirt?
What does the moon whisper?
Is hate a person who robs us of our will?
Are bird, beast, stone and star all one?
What is love?
Is dog mankind's friend?
What language does the wind speak?
What is the language of the sunlight and stars?

HEATHER REESE
Grade 4, Hawthorne Elementary
Poet Teacher: Veronica Cunningham
Teacher: Ann MacDonald

The Eagle

I am an eagle
an angel
a scream of freedom
and bravery
gliding around the earth
I believe
in me
my dreams
in the past

CHAZ NEWSOM
Grade 4, John Adams Elementary
Poet-Teacher: Steve Garber
Teacher: Jill Hall

Nighthand

Not day,
not light.
It's night,
and it has thousands of twinkling stars
like millions of grains of white rice on
a frying pan. Night is
like a giant black hand
holding earth and planets like marbles.

PETER KEHRLI
Grade 7, Standley Jr. High
Poet-Teacher: Brandon Cesmat
Teacher: Bob Frain

Indigo Rain

When indigo sings like rain
I am discontent.
Voices overlap like fresh sheets.
On the white cliffs of Dover,
we become one in eternity.

When circles become spheres
I am in-between,
lost among dimensions of my world.

When cats sleep beneath the night
I am alone,
lost in the disembodied green
dancing in their eyes.

When one becomes two
we are shallow in our discourse.
The pages of lives long past
are erased in vain.

Indigo rain is all there is.
In each drop is a reflection of heaven,
carried down through the cosmos.
My hazel eyes reflect daylight
as the moon appears over the naked cliffs.

JOHN UNRUH
Grade 10, Scripps Ranch High
Poet-Teacher: Celia Sigmon
Teacher: Chris Dickerson

Just a Body

Mine is a heart stripped naked like the moon
Alone, moving only because it has to.
It is quiet because it has no love to speak of.
Its aspirations are left behind in heel prints.
It is just a body that walks for no reason,
With no more desire than a ghost.

Where is the eagle that will pick it up
With drinking wings and swallow the hail
Of thunder before striking,
Unprotected?

Probably it is flying a starless sky,
Lost and directionless,
Like my heart.

MEGAN SULLIVAN
Grade 10, Scripps Ranch High
Poet-Teacher: Joe Milosch
Teacher: Chris Dickerson

The Battle of the Tigers

I come from a small family
of the greatest beast of them all.
With my stripes I came forward
in a battle against the Siberians.
The Siberian tigers, the famous relative
of our little Bengal group.

The general asked for volunteers.
I came forward with my glaring eyes.
My determination leaned only toward the rebel,
and I charged my enemy,
the Siberian tiger, the greater tiger.

I swiped with my mighty claws,
and I landed once or twice.
I kept charging forward,
showing my shiny teeth.
I did the impossible,
I caught up with him.
Now I tear him apart and eat his meat.

Later, I feel guilty
that I killed
such a worthy opponent.

JAMIE GODLEY
Grade 5, La Mesa Dale
Poet-Teacher: Joe Milosch
Teacher: Charlotte Bauer

Candle

A high mountain
Sitting in a frozen lake.
In the top there is a bright tear blown by the wind.

JOSE LUIS SANDOVAL
Grade 7, National City Middle
Poet-Teacher: Roxanne Young
Teacher: Laura Marugg

Thunderhead

Anger like thunder
striking you in the head
and telling you to be angry like
a tornado turning in your brain and
mixing you up like a flood of
rain filling your head with an earthquake
shaking good things out
like fog covering your head
with anger and black sky
that can't help you see any good thing

NANCY MORALES
Grade 4, Pauma
Poet-Teacher: Brandon Cesmat
Teacher: Katherine Mancino

The Lioness

I am a female lion out in the grasslands
catching food for my mate.
Every day I do this,
I catch a feast for my mate,
and my brothers and husband lie around and wait.
While females run across the grassland
catching a feast for them,
the females dodge traps that men set.

And then the males eat first,
so that we and the children are left with a lesser ration,
but we eat up so that our hunger is filled.
Then the next day we go out again.
Why do the males have to be so lazy and demanding?
We'll never know.

AMANDA THOMAS
Grade 5, La Mesa Dale Elementary
Poet-Teacher: Joe Milosch
Teacher: Marty Rinze

Wolf

I am Wolf
My freedom but a remembrance,
a fond memory
I recall the free tundra
where I live
Only
In my restless dreams
All hope
seems lost
I am trapped
Cold Iron Walls
that bind me,
keep me
from the wild tundra,
My last candle
of Hope
flickered out
this morning
I woke to find
my family in my sight
I could not reach them . . .
The monsters that hold me here
have stripped me of
the right
to die
on the tundra
or become
part
of another animal
Alone . . .
I desperately want to go
HOME
The great powers of Loneliness are vast.

LYNDA J. B. BROWNING
Grade 6, Muirlands Middle
Poet-Teacher: Steve Garber
Teacher: Richard Gray

Red

Red,
Rooted,
In a diamond sea,
A rare flower,
With flames,
Spearing in every direction,
Like a double-edged sword.

BRIAN CALIMLIM
Grade 9, Standley Jr. High
Poet-Teacher: Joe Milosch
Teacher: Rob Larson

"I Am a Cerise Tiger" / Anna Heinrichs / Grade 10, Point Loma High School

Dragons Weep Diamonds

Sometimes walking late at night,
I imagine I am riding
a dragon.
Before she goes, she leaves me
something
to remember her by:
a hard, clear rock,
the size of my fist,
a dragon's tear.

Sometimes walking late at night,
clutching my dragon's tear,
I remember her parting words,
"Dragons weep diamonds."

Sometimes walking late at night,
I look toward the stars.
I murmur,
"I cry tears of sorrow."

Sometimes walking late at night,
I think of my dragon.
While clutching her tear,
I remember,
"Dragons weep diamonds."

JULIE NIEN-YUAN WU
Grade 8, Standley Jr. High
Poet-Teacher: Roxanne Young
Teacher: Sally Owen

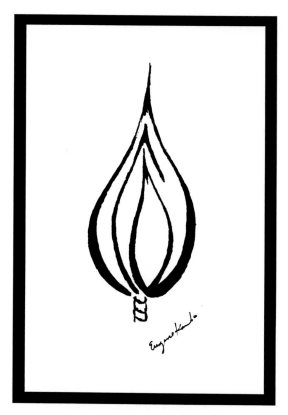

"The Flame" / Eugene Kaneko / Grade 11, Scripps Ranch High

The Phoenix's Bride

The flame that danced on the wax
Never still and never lax
Like the beautiful Phoenix's bride
All so bright it can not hide

Like a ghost on top a hill
It jumped around and was never still
Yet it gives off light
That is oh so bright

Like a shining nymph that dances
Or a lancer's shining lances
Everywhere danced round and round
Still there wasn't any sound

The flames they leapt into the air
And lit the face of Balinet's hair
The sword on his lap, like a star
Shined so brightly from afar

Quietly we all looked on the flame
The flame that never was the same
As on it danced round and round
There still wasn't any sound

ADRIAN MILIK
Grade 7, Standley Jr. High
Poet-Teacher: Roxanne Young
Teacher: Wendy Cobb

Comezón de Paz

Me da comezón en mi corazón para ir al bosque y
vivir en una casa hecha de adobe donde uno puede llegar a pie
con los árboles grandes como un gigante
y el camino lleno de tierra y peidras.
La casa enterrada como un poro en la tierra durmiendo y
hay paredes con curvas de una cebolla.
Descansando de la gente ocupada
con las pensamientos de las ciudades del mundo.

The Itch for Peace

My heart itches to go into the wilderness,
to live in an adobe house
where one's feet could lead on walks
through trees big as giants
on a rocky dirt road.
The house's doorway will be like a pore
in the face of the sleeping earth,
the walls with curves like an onion's.
A place resting from people busy
with thoughts of the cities around the world.

ANACELLY QUINTANA
Grade 11, Kearny High
Poet-Teacher: Brandon Cesmat
Teacher: Virginia Sánchez-Bernardy

Silence

Silence all I hear,
silence all I fear,
seems to sneak up on me.
It always has.
You might say I am crazy to fear it,
but I fear what can come after it.
Thoughts race through my body.

It could strike me at any minute,
only, as quick as it came
it could go.
I don't know how anyone can sleep through it,
but maybe it won't get me.
Then, again, maybe it could.

I had a daydream, and the monster
it represented was two steps behind me.
Through the alleys and streets I ran.
It never could catch me, but the point is,
I kept running.

Maybe it was my mortality growing near
that I feared.
Sad, but true, it almost caught me,
No matter what I threw at it.
it was too relentless to stop.

In case you're still wondering
what I am afraid of,
it is thunder.
It can be known by any name,
but to me it will be Banshee,
Messenger of Death,
the Feared One.

CHRISTOPHER LEE SADDLER
Grade 8, Standley Jr. High
Poet-Teacher: minerva
Teacher: Sally Owen

If I Were,
Would You Care?

If only you could understand
    I wouldn't have to hide.
If only I were darkness
    I would lure you to my shadowy secret underworld.
But none of that matters anymore.
My love for you is not good enough.
If only I could open your eyes
    what would you see and would you appreciate it?
If only I could gather my courage and tell you that I care
    instead of hiding in this poem.
If I gave you love, would you give some back?
If I wasn't such a shy and cowardly person
    would I have the courage to tell you I even like you?
If only I could tell you
    whom I was addressing!
If I were blue
    would you love me more?
If I were a smack
    would you hear me kiss you?
If I were a squirrel
    I'd steal your love and give some back.

If I were water I'd trickle
down every perfect curve of your body.
If I were two
would you love me twice as much?
If I were any deadly disease
I'd rather die before I hurt you.
If I were a BMW
would you still love me for who I am?
If I were a summer day
I'd wait forever to see you in a bathing suit.
If I were spring
I'd make you enjoy every day of that season.
If I were Aladdin
I'd want you to be my Jasmine.
But I'm afraid that all of this will never come true,
for I am scared to admit who you are to the world,
let alone to you.
But would you care?

DAVID SIEV
Grade 9, Standley Jr. High
Poet-Teacher: Celia Sigmon
Teacher: Norma Fox

Black and White

White is the color of truth . . . the scent of freshly-baked cookies.

Black is the sight of a young puppy's life being drawn out through fear, seconds before it is struck with a bat by an angry child.

White. The color that surrounds my baby sister's face. She glows . . . as if an angel . . . she is an angel.

Black is the taste of the sticky licorice left on my baby sister's fingers as she shoves them in my mouth.

White is the satin feel of cold milk sliding down my throat, filling me with comfort and wiriness.

Black is how I see the future of the ignorant. In black coffins, nails bleeding from scraping the cold roof until the last, wishful breath is taken.

White is the flash of light I see before the memory of being at my mother's breast, my mouth over her nipple, drinking her love.

Black smells like burned flesh, cremation . . . death.

White is the child untouched by ignorance, first born, still innocent. The child still loving all who are friendly, not judging weight, color, race, beauty, or ugliness.

Black are the sounds of pain, the screams of agony.

White . . . my joy, my happiness . . . the sound of my lover's heartbeat when I rest my head on his chest. White . . . are the last days of my life when I go to heaven.

Of these two colors, whether sweet or bitter, I dream most of the precious white of my African . . . "Black" . . . soul.

NIKKI DOUGLAS
Grade 11, Twain Beach
Poet-Teacher: Joe Milosch
Teacher: Stephanie Mendenhall

An Unwilling Acceptance

We all fall into a beast when we are born
Whether we like it or not
Some are perfectly content with it
Some despise it

It comes to me like a shadow of something awful
A grave figure coming out of the dark
And approaching me

Like a doctor telling me my desires have passed away
Now being forced into a disguised dictatorship
Carrying out the hopes and dreams of other people
Personal hopes and dreams

Like being free to travel
And discover things that are beautiful
Like a secret spot in the forest
That no one knows about
Should overpower the dreams of others

We should live like the animals that we are
Being in touch with their own greatness
Instead we live held on a tight leash
And made to obey

If we don't we are shamed
"Told that we will never be anything"
Most don't even realize what is happening
They just follow along with it

And worry about which business they will enter
Never thinking about what they would rather be doing
I think about it sometimes
And it seems impossible

TONY ADRIGNOLA
Grade 9, Serra High
Poet-Teacher: Joe Milosch
Teacher: Arlene Gruber

Sorrow

The color of sorrow is the clear crystal blue of a drop,
    falling from the face of a cold, frozen glacier.
It longs to be the taste to cool, sobering water
    rinsing away all troubled thoughts.
In reality, it is the dull burn of the third shot
    of brandy that hour.
It embodies the sound of the quiet morning of a child
    not quite understanding why to weep
      for the death of a dear friend.
The very small of the salty tears trickling down a tired child's cheek.
    Sorrow is a great lonely massif to see, yet too terrifying to climb.
      It is the feeling of being like a memory of childhood times
        lost and forgotten
      at the bottom of an elegant bottle of wine.

GRACE M. JARRETT
Grade 11, Valhalla High
Poet-Teacher: Joe Milosch
Teacher: Claire Tremaine

Backfire

I'm gloomy and full of darkness,
    one point to aim.
I bring pain and suffering
    with one pull.
I take away the precious things
    belonging to others.
Some use me to solve their problems
    when I only make them worse.
When I am in your hand,
    you feel as if you're on top,
but when you look into my hole,
    you see yourself at the end of the world.
Every tick of the clock, a tear falls
    because of me.
Never have me
    in your hand.

TUYEN LE
Grade 8, Standley Jr. High
Poet-Teacher: Brandon Cesmat
Teacher: Jim Harris

"Monolith" / Joaquin Tena

Ice

Encased in a lucite block,
frozen forever in time,
a beast locked in a clear cold coffin,
a scorpion caught in ice.

Claws frozen outstretched,
tail curved, ready to attack.
Legs forever scrambling,
he's forever still.

Closed tight in a box,
the little beast isn't so bad.
Yet to meet him in the open,
scuttling swiftly across the sand
is painful:
he's a poison too potent to bear.

A scorpion in my memory
frozen like my mind.
That beast
of a stepparent
who has lost all
his power over me,
is now encased,
frozen forever, poised to attack,
and at the tip
of his colored tail,
a brief, black stinger.

BRYAN LUDWIG
Grade 12, Crawford High
Poet-Teacher: Joe Milosch
Teacher: Robin Visconti

Eyeballs

In my coffin, I see spiders
eating my head and brain.
My eyes are good, so I can see
everything I want to see in my life,
but I know I am dead from a car
hitting me on my bicycle.
All they had left when they scraped me
from the road were my skin and head
that they put in a small rock coffin,
green as emerald rock.
The spiders got in just in time.

In another hundred years,
when they open that green rock box,
all that will be left are my eyes and bones.
My eyes will be alive the rest of earth's years,
and when the earth explodes,
my eyes will go on a long journey,
seeing everything they can
until all disintegrates into little pieces
that can never be put together again.
After my eyes rot, I will never exist.

JOEL MENDENHALL
Grade 5, Palomar Mountain
Poet-Teacher: Brandon Cesmat
Teacher: Ellen Humphrey

If

If I was a trigger
would you pull me?
If I was a cigar
would you light me up?
If I was dirty
would you clean me?
If I was an ant
would you step on me?
If I was dead
would you miss me?
If I was a baby
would you kiss me?
If I was food
would you eat me?
Well then,
  pull
  light
  clean
  step
  miss
  kiss
  eat.
Do something.
If I was a human
would you love me
or would you hate me?
Why?

ANTHONY NAVARRO
Grade 9, Standley Jr. High
Poet-Teacher: Celia Sigmon
Teacher: Norma Fox

Oso Temblor

El está acostado
en una cama chica.

En el cuarto alumbrado,
no se le nota ni una arruga en al cara.

Por esta bien acobijado del frío,
parece un oso.

Temblando del frío,
parece que esta pasando por un temblor.

Earthquake Bear

He lies on
a small bed.

In the lighted room,
you don't notice a wrinkle on his face.

Because he is covered with blankets from the cold,
he looks like a big bear.

Shivering from the cold,
it seems as if he is passing through an earthquake.

Purificación Sánchez
Grade 4, Pauma
Poet-Teacher: Brandon Cesmat
Teacher: Catherine Mancino

Listen!

It's not over till I say it is.
Hey! I'm important too!
When I want you to quit,
believe me, I'll say so!
I'm not giving up,
not gonna jump off my own cliff.
Don't push me down,
when I stand up.
Don't tell me to leave,
when I open my mouth.
I want my voice heard!
And what if the things I say
turn your face a raspberry hue?
Who cares?
Don't prick me with a needle.
Don't be my mother.
Don't crowd me with a whir of dirty gray clouds.
I'll be heard,
'cuz it's not over till I say it is.

HEIDI BUCK
Grade 10, Point Loma High
Poet-Teacher: Glory Foster
Teacher: Rosemarie Smith

The Hourglass

The twisted waters of time
Drifting in and falling down
To the depths of salty land
Sighing, swaying through the earth
Sands of time are seeping
Never to be seen again
Memories but sleeping
Drifting down into the sky
Falling into space
Time means nothing to the earth
Curved horizons make no line.

ELIZABETH CAIN
Grade 9, Helix High
Poet-Teacher: Jana Gardner
Teacher: Jessica Patton

Marina Morrow
Grade 12, Scripps Ranch High

DISTINGUISHED RUNNERS UP

Challenger Junior High School
Mary Tran, "I Am"

Clear View Elementary School
Heidi Peterson, "Peace of the Soul"
Emily B. Taylor, "Questions of the Shadows"

Crawford High School
Morgan Ryan Clabaugh, "The Music"

Hawthorne Elementary School
Matthew Barrs, "On My Mind"
Sara Chazin, "Brown"
Minna Chen, "Light Purple"
Jasmine Lai, "Blank Paper"
Hillary Ruggles, "Why Ask Why?"

Highland Ranch Elementary School
Amy Nugent, "Flying"
Stephanie Waidelich, "Riding the Wind"

John Adams Elementary School
Paul Estrada, "Lion"
Iona Maranger, "Back to Me"
Nicholas David Rentflejs, "I Am a Bald Eagle"

Keiller Middle School
Crystal Farnbach, "On That Grim Day"
Macale Herschel, "Dinosaurs"
Joseph B. Johnson, "Why Can't?"
Sam Ly, "Oysters and Breezy Harps"
Valencia Yerania, "In My Country"

Lindbergh/Schweitzer Elementary School
Alisha Cooke, "Me"

Mark Twain High School
John Rivera, "My Hendrix Experience"

Miramar Ranch Elementary School
Kerry Ono Vineberg, "Dust"

Muirlands Middle School
Sara Clopton, "Leaf on the Ground"
Rebecca Maescher, "Children Wish"

National City Middle School
Janella Curtis, "The Country Road"
Kimberly Galindo, "Dare to Dream"
Liz Cassler, "A Special Locket"
Annabelle Gonzales, "Garden Flowers"
Vanessa Gutierrez, "Teddy Bear"

Olive Pierce Middle School
Suzanne Arena, Untitled
Chrissy Kapelczak, "Trapped"
Cody Ramsey, "Step"

Pacific Beach Elementary School
Jessi Johnson, "Meadow in Me"
Corbin Prychun, "The Emperor's Rice"

Palomar Mountain School
Jacqueline Ravenscroft, "Skyhorse"

Point Loma High School
Damien Schiff, "A Bit of This"
Lisa Wong, "Green"

Samuel F. B. Morse High School
Justin Berger, "Tenement of Life"

San Diego Community Home School
Cole Gabaldon, "Ice Cream Every Day"

San Pasqual Union School
Abby Wolanyk, "Against the Thunder"

Scripps Ranch High School
Christopher Irwin, Untitled
Steve Salmon, "The Ring"

Serra High School
Sara Adamek, "Ode to Sugar"
Lisa Kingery, "Artwork"

Spreckels Elementary School
Sarah Jane Lambert, "The Wind"

Standley Junior High School
Richard Coughran, "I Am"
Oliva Frost, "While Looking at Fireworks"
Rachel Hetzel, "Doll Poem"
Marina Javor, "Dry Music"
Chris Johnson, "Voices"
AnnaLee Kronenberg, "Cloudless"
Kuster Daeson, "Low Riders"
Michelle Landau, "This Blue Rock"
Marc Lessem, "If I Were a Cave"
Shery Nazerpour, "I Am..."
Elizabeth Padilla, "A Nineties Child"
Lauren Patella, "Dream Maker"
Tony Sisouvanh, "Music"
Robert Vonguilay, "So Much Darkness"
Shalonda Waines, "I Am..."

Twain Beach
Liz Cassler, "A Special Locket"

Valhalla High School
Roxy Easter, "Hasta La Vista, Baby"
Katharine Nye, "Blue Box"

HONORABLE MENTIONS

Balboa Elementary School
Joni Malabrigo, "Racing Horse"

Challenger Junior High School
Marilyn Guro, "Who, What, Where and Why"

Clear View Elementary School
Chanel N. Chandler, "Our Dreams Are"
Peter Girten, "One Wonderful Thing"

Emerald Middle School
Jason Brown, "Stars"
Desiree Thompson, "Rain From Heaven"

Fred Baker Elementary School
Jessica Bice, "What I'd Like to Be"
Lily Phosaath, "I Am..."

Helix High School
Inessa Shalomov, "Alone"

Highland Ranch Elementary School
Mallory Kozar, "Connection"

John Adams Elementary School
Julia Yvette Angulo, "I Am"
Cheryl Clements, "Life as a Tear"
Lina Karaoglanova, "I Am a Flower"

Keiller Middle School
Maria Alejandrino, "Trapped"
Crystal Farnbach,
    "Looking Through the Window"
Herschell Macale, "Dinosaurs"
Ariana Munoz, "Loved One's Death"
Cynthia Webb, "In Another World"

La Mesa Dale Elementary School
Christina Shu, "Horse"

Lindbergh/Schweitzer Elementary School
Megan Archer, "Flame"
Marissa Moncrief, "The Flame"
Nathaniel Morgan, "Wise Wolf"

Monte Vista High School
Erik Mendez, "The Rock Versus the Flame"
Jessica Steinert, "Candle Romance"

Muirlands Middle School
Georgina Garcia, "I Am a Lamp"
Melissa Li, "Red Tide"
Yuanxin Zhou, "The Flame of Passion"

National City Middle School
Linda Acosta, "Someone Sees My Eyes"
Myrtha Anaya, "Tears from the World"

Olive Pierce Middle School
Amber Aguilera, "If I Were a Soccer Field"

Pacific Beach Elementary School
Brandon Reed, "The Oak Outside"
Paul Tagariello, "Swimming"

Palomar Mountain School
Rachel Ann Baker, "Melody of Love"
Kaitlyn Swenson, "Black, Tan, White and Dry"

Pauma School
Rio Reyes, "Bloody Face"

Point Loma High School
Christina Snell, "Red"

Scripps Ranch High School
Scott Hinkle, "The T.V."
Kelly Varonfakis, "I Am Gold"
Jessica Warner, "The New Light"

San Diego Community Home School
Beth Gergurich, "Thieves"

Spreckels Elementary School
Barbara Edwards, "Desert Bloom"

Standley Junior High School
Daiske Beppu, "Pumas Around the World"
Staci Berman, "Laugh in the Rain"
Teneshia Davis, "Dreams"
Grant Donovan, "Flying"
Nickie DuVall, "Staples"
Nancy Ebrahimi, "I Am..."
Hessy Field, "Poetry"
Claudia Juarez, "Where I Come From!"
Crystall Kean, "Soaring Teddy"
Laura Kuczenski, "Full Page"
Joshua McLean, "Pumas Around the World"
Kelly McNeal, "Bud , My Frog"
Dana Stueland, "School"
Esteban Tirado, "Why?"

Twain Beach School
Joaquin Tena, "Cat"

Valhalla High School
Daryl Green, "Peeling Down"
Kenny C. Smith, "Bumper Sticker"